Kudus

Victoria Blakemore

vblakemore.author@gmail.com

Copyright info/picture credits

Cover, Christopher Reusch/Shutterstock; Page 3, ondrejprosicky/AdobeStock; Page 5, Jurgens/AdobeStock; Page 7, Dewald/AdobeStock; Page 9, Stephen/Adobestock; Pages 10-11, Handmade Pictures/AdobeStock; Page 13, JohanSwanepoel/AdobeStock; Page 15, Nick Dale/AdobeStock; Page 17, Australian Stock/AdobeStock; Page 19, Aberson/AdobeStock; Page 21, gallas/AdobeStock; Page 23; Bernhard Bekker/AdobeStock; Page 25, PACO COMO/AdobeStock; Page 27, ronnybas/AdobeStock; Page 29, RoyA/AdobeStock; Page 31, Bernhard Bekker/AdobeStock; Page 33, Christopher Reusch/Shutterstock

Table of Contents

What Are Kudus?

Kudus are mammals that are part of the antelope family. They are also related to animals such as sheep, goats, and buffalo.

There are two kinds of kudus: the greater kudu and the lesser kudu. They differ in size and the number of white stripes they have on their back.

Greater kudus are larger than lesser kudus. They also have fewer white stripes and a throat **mane.**

Size

Lesser kudus grow to be around 3 feet tall. Adults usually weigh between 130 and 230 pounds.

Greater kudus are much larger than lesser kudus. They can grow to be over 5 feet tall and weigh between 260 and 600 pounds.

Male kudus are usually larger

than female kudus.

Physical Characteristics

Kudus are tan, brown, and white in color. Their coloring and white stripes work as **camouflage**. They are able to blend in with the grasses and dirt of their habitat.

Kudus have large, rounded ears that they can turn. This allows them to hear things such as **predators** from far away.

Male kudus have large, twisted horns. Their horns are usually less than four feet long, but have been known to grow up to six feet.

Habitat

Kudus live in areas with lots of **brush**. Woodlands, hills, and mountains are all homes to kudus.

They prefer areas with lots of plants so that plenty of food is available. Kudus do not need to live close to water.

Kudus are found in parts of

South and East Africa.

They live in countries such as Namibia, Ethiopia, Tanzania, Kenya, and South Africa.

Diet

Kudus are **herbivores**. This means that they eat only plants.

Their diet is made up of plant parts such as leaves, shoots, and roots. They have also been known to eat fruits when they can find them.

Kudus usually do most of their **foraging** at dusk and dawn when it is cooler.

Kudus are known as **browsers**. This means that they eat plant parts such as leaves, stems, and flowers. They do not usually eat grasses like **grazers**.

They get most of their water from the plants they eat. This allows them to live in areas where it is hot and dry.

Kudus rarely need to drink water. They can live in places where water is **scarce**.

Communication

Kudus use mainly sound and movement to communicate with each other.

Kudus have excellent hearing. When something startles them, they lift their tail to flash the white fur underneath. This alerts other kudus of possible danger.

Kudus can be very loud! They

make a sharp barking sound.

It can be used to warn others

of danger nearby.

Movement

Kudus spend most of their time browsing and foraging for food. They do most of their running to stay safe from **predators** such as hyenas, lions, and African wild dogs.

Kudus have been known to run over fifty miles per hour when needed.

Kudus are very **agile** and can jump very high. They have been known to jump over things that were eight feet tall!

Kudu Calves

Kudus usually have one baby, or calf. When they are first born, calves stay hidden in the tall grasses to stay safe from **predators**.

After a few weeks, calves are able to join the herd.

Calves stay with their mothers

for over a year before leaving

to find a new herd.

Kudu Life

Kudus may life alone or in small groups that are called herds. Most herds are made up of mothers and calves.

Kudus are active in the evening and early morning when it is cooler. It is also easier for them to hide from **predators** when it isn't as bright out.

Kudus are usually very peaceful.

However, males sometimes fight

over mates by locking horns,

Lifespan

In the wild, kudus can live between ten and fifteen years. In **captivity**, kudus can often live over twenty years.

Many wild kudus don't survive past the age of three. This is due to disease and being hunted by **predators**.

Population

Greater kudu populations are **stable** on private and protected lands. Their populations are **decreasing** in the wild.

Lesser kudu populations are also **decreasing** in the wild. There are fewer lesser kudus than greater kudus in the wild.

Lesser kudus are listed as near threatened. They could be in trouble if their populations continues to **decrease**.

Kudus in Danger

While kudu populations are not currently in trouble, they are facing some dangers from humans.

Kudu habitats are being destroyed for farming, buildings, and roads. There are fewer safe places for kudus to live in the wild.

Kudus are often hunted for their meat, horns, and **hides**. Their horns are used for musical instruments and hunting trophies.

Helping Kudus

Kudus are not currently in danger of becoming **extinct**, but people are still trying to help them.

Many places have hunting laws that protect animals such as kudus. These laws limit when and how many animals can be hunted.

There are **preserves** in parts of Africa where animals like kudus live. These special protected lands are safe places for animals to live. Kudus that live there are safe from hunting and habitat destruction.

Kudu populations in these areas are **increasing**. This is good news for the future of the kudus.

Glossary

Browser: an animal that feeds on plant parts such as leaves, shoots, and fruits

Brush: bushes, shrubs, and small trees that are close to the ground in a forest or woodland

Camouflage: using color to blend in to the surroundings

Captivity: animals that are kept by humans, not in the wild

Decrease: to get smaller

Decreasing: getting smaller

Extinct: when there are no more of an animal left in the wild

Foraging: looking for food

Grazing: when animals eat grass

Herbivores: animals that eat only plants

Hides: animal skins

Increase: to get bigger

Mane: an area of long hair on an animal's

neck

Predator: an animal that hunts other animals

for food

Preserves: areas of land set up to protect

plants and animals

Scarce: when there isn't much of something

Stable: steady, not likely to change

About the Author

Victoria Blakemore is a first grade

teacher in Southwest Florida with a

passion for reading.

You can visit her at

www.elementaryexplorers.com

Also in This Series

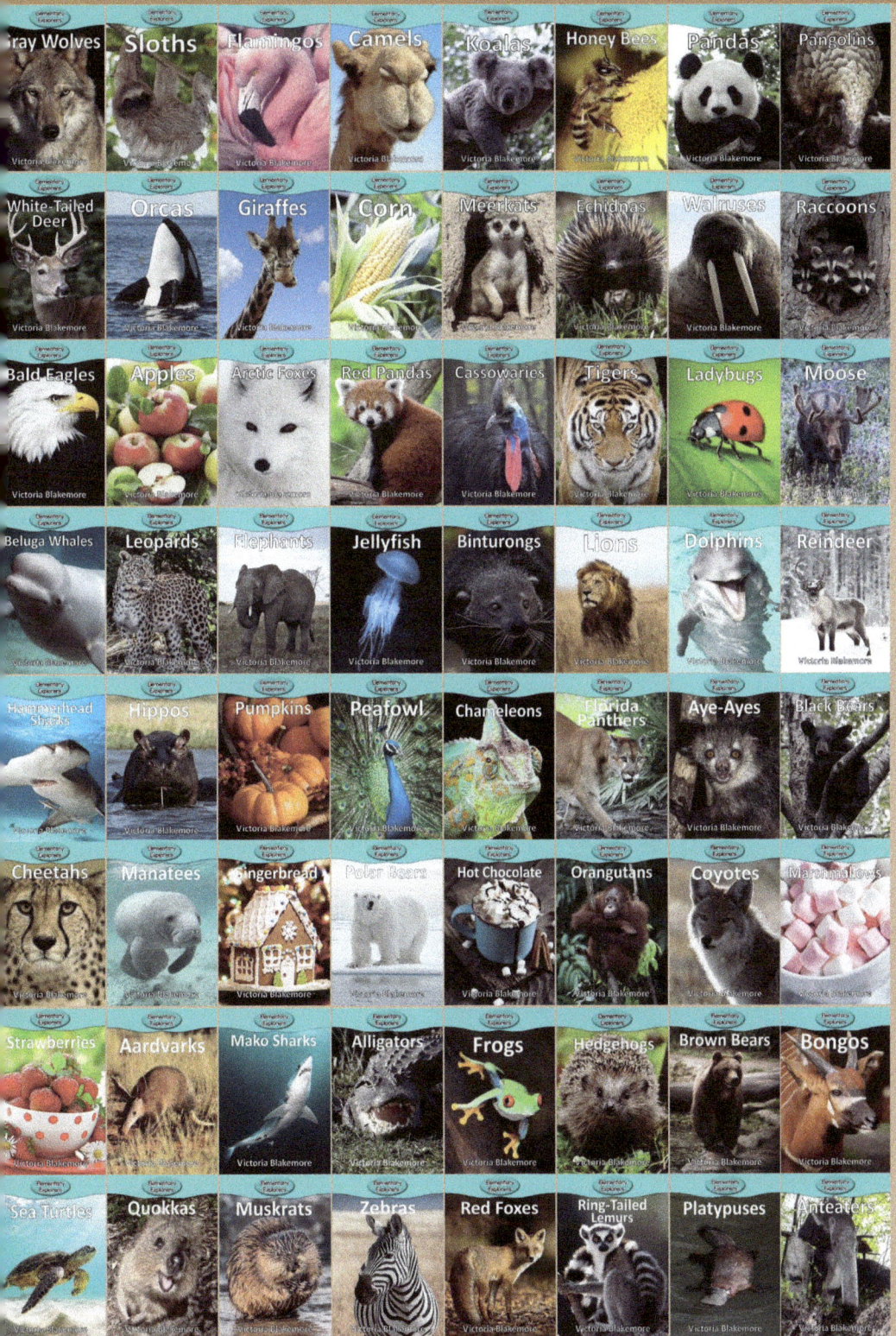

Also in This Series

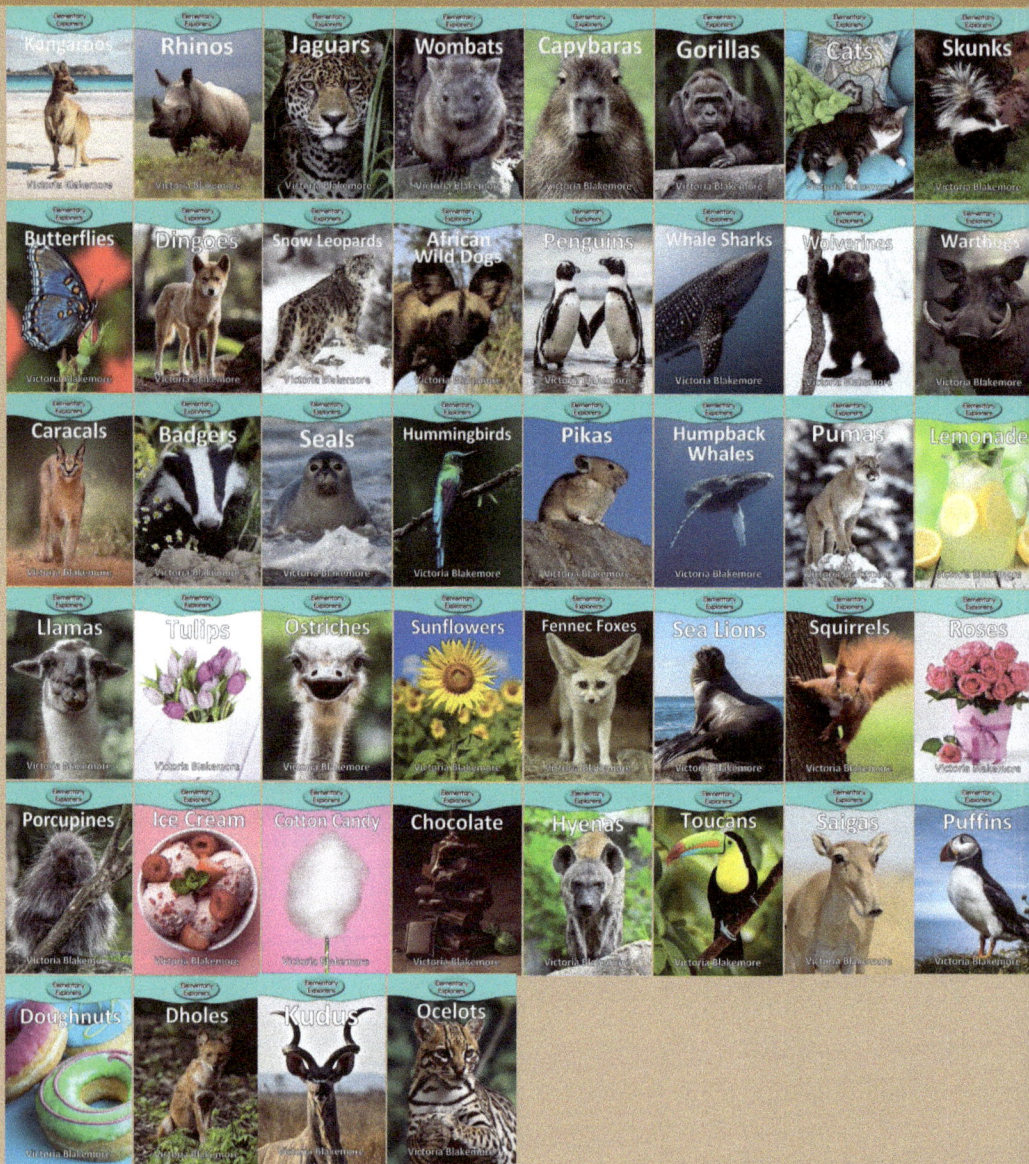

Kangaroos
Rhinos
Jaguars
Wombats
Capybaras
Gorillas
Cats
Skunks

Butterflies
Dingoes
Snow Leopards
African Wild Dogs
Penguins
Whale Sharks
Wolverines
Warthogs

Caracals
Badgers
Seals
Hummingbirds
Pikas
Humpback Whales
Pumas
Lemonade

Llamas
Tulips
Ostriches
Sunflowers
Fennec Foxes
Sea Lions
Squirrels
Roses

Porcupines
Ice Cream
Cotton Candy
Chocolate
Hyenas
Toucans
Saigas
Puffins

Doughnuts
Dholes
Kudus
Ocelots

www.ingramcontent.com/pod-product-compliance
Lightning Source LLC
Chambersburg PA
CBHW052124030426
42335CB00025B/3110